SYSTEMS OF POWER:

RUSSIA

Sonya Newland

Franklin Watts
First published in Great Britain in 2020 by The Watts Publishing Group
Copyright © The Watts Publishing Group, 2020

Produced for Franklin Watts by
White-Thomson Publishing Ltd
www.wtpub.co.uk

Credits
Editor: Sonya Newland
Designer: Dan Prescott, Couper Street Type Co.
Consultant: Philip Parker
Illustrations: TechType (4)

The publisher would like to thank the following for permission to reproduce their pictures:
Alamy: World History Archive 8, IanDagnall Computing 9t, Shawshot 9b, Pictorial Press Ltd
10, Hum Historical 13t, dpa picture alliance 13b, Nikolay Vinokurov 17, ITAR-TASS News
Agency 18t, 20, 21b, 25b, 37t, 39t, PhotoXpress/ZUMAPRESS.com 21t, ITAR-TASS/ Alexandra
Mudrats 23t, Xinhua 31t, 43t, O. Kravets/Focuspictures/ASK 31b, ZUMA Press, Inc. 35t, Russian
Government 41t, Foto Arena LTDA 42; The Russian Presidential Press and Information Office:
cover right; Shutterstock: Moroz Yurii cover left, bissig cover middle, Alexey Broslavets 5t,
Tatiana Grozetskaya 5b, withGod 6, OlegDoroshin 7, Everett Historical 11, 360b 12, Konstantin
Gushcha 14t, Roman Sibiryakov 14b, SSV-Studio 15t, Alesem 15b, Tatiana Gasich 16, Free
Wind 2014 18b, 38, Rostislav Ageev 19, Northfoto 22, Starikov Pavel 23b, ID1974 24, Max
kolomychenko 25t, StockphotoVideo 26, Altstock Productions 27t, photo.ua 27b, Kekyalyaynen
28, hlopex 29t, Evgeny Vorobyev 29b, Georg Spade 30, Sergei Butorin 32, Farhad Sadykov
33t, amadeustx 33b, Vladimir Gappov 34, Vasil Kuzmichonak 35b, Jonas Petrovas 36, De Visu
37b, nexus 7 39b, plavevski 40, A_Lesik 41b, Amani A 43b, Fotosr52 44, shinobi 45.

All design elements from Shutterstock.

Every attempt has been made to clear copyright. Should there be any
inadvertent omission please apply to the publisher for rectification.

Printed in Malaysia

Franklin Watts
An imprint of
Hachette Children's Group
Part of The Watts Publishing Group
Carmelite House
50 Victoria Embankment
London EC4Y 0DZ

An Hachette UK Company
www.hachette.co.uk
www.franklinwatts.co.uk

CONTENTS

WHAT makes Russia unique?   4

WHAT political system does Russia have?   6

HOW was Russia governed in the past?   8

WHY did communism end?   12

HOW is the government structured?   16

WHO is Vladimir Putin?   20

WHO is Dmitry Medvedev?   24

WHAT are today's key challenges?   26

WHY are environmental issues important?   28

WHAT resources does Russia have?   30

WHAT about the economy?   32

WHAT is Russia's nuclear status?   34

WHAT about human rights?   36

HOW does Russia exert a global influence?   38

WHAT are Russia's international relations like?   40

WHAT lies ahead?   44

Glossary   46

Further information   47

Index   48

Russia is a vast country – the largest in the world. At 17,098,242 square km, it covers nearly twice the area of the second-largest country, Canada. Governing a nation so big that it spans two continents, Europe and Asia, and covers 11 time zones, brings many challenges.

NEAR NEIGHBOURS

Russia has a lot of coastline, including 24,140 km along the Arctic Ocean in the north. But its large size also means that the main landmass shares borders with 12 other countries, making it second only to China in terms of border countries. Over the years, Russia's borders have shifted as territory has changed hands through war and conflict. Protecting, and sometimes expanding, the country's borders has been a key concern for Russian leaders.

Most of the Russian population is focused in the European areas in the west. Fewer people live in the mountainous regions and the colder eastern parts of the country such as Siberia.

THE RUSSIAN PEOPLE

Despite its huge land area, Russia ranks ninth in the world in terms of population, with an estimated 144 million people. Although nearly 81 per cent of the population is Russian, people from around 185 other national or ethnic groups also live there. Despite its ethnic diversity, Russia is one of the few countries in the world experiencing what experts call a 'negative growth rate'. This means that more people are leaving Russia, either by dying or emigrating, than are being born or moving there from other countries.

★ More than 11.5 million people live in the capital city, Moscow.

A WEALTH OF RESOURCES

Russia has huge reserves of natural resources, but this has proved both a blessing and a curse. Having the biggest mining industry in the world has the potential to bring the country enormous wealth. However, Russia relies on this industry almost entirely – and that makes the country vulnerable. If global prices drop, the effect on the Russian economy can be devastating. Russian leaders are looking for ways to reduce their reliance on natural resources.

★ This is the Mir diamond mine in Siberia. Russia's natural resources are worth an estimated US$75 trillion.

CHANGING TIMES

Few countries have experienced such dramatic changes to their systems of power as Russia did in the twentieth century. Throughout this period, the country moved from being an autocratic monarchy to a communist state. Towards the end of the century, communism was overturned. The democratic system established in the 1990s drew Russia closer to other democracies and allowed it to become a significant force on the world stage.

SYSTEM DOES RUSSIA HAVE?

The political system in Russia today is known as a 'federal semi-presidential republic'. This sounds complicated, but in fact it just means that it has a president and a prime minister who both have responsibilities in running the country.

WHO CHOOSES?

Lots of countries have semi-presidential systems, although the way that the leaders are chosen is not always the same. For example, in France and Poland, parliament chooses the prime minister. In Russia, the president chooses the prime minister and other senior officials. Having two people in charge might seem like a good balance of power, but in reality it's not that simple. Semi-presidential systems can operate in different ways – and sometimes the president wields a lot more power than the prime minister.

Everyone over the age of 18 is entitled to vote in Russia.

'I pledge to respect and protect the rights and liberties of every citizen; to observe and protect the Constitution of the Russian Federation; to protect the sovereignty and independence, security and integrity of the state and to serve the people faithfully.'

Oath sworn by every president of Russia

PICKING THE PRESIDENT

The president of Russia is the head of state. Presidents are elected by the Russian people. If one candidate does not win 50 per cent or more of the vote (an absolute majority), a second round of voting takes place in which the top two candidates go head to head. Presidential elections are held every six years, and a president is limited to two consecutive terms. However, there is nothing stopping someone running for president again after a term out of office.

PRESIDENTIAL DUTIES

Officially, the president's duties are to uphold the constitution and to protect the rights of the Russian people. The president defines the country's domestic and foreign policy, and is commander-in-chief of the armed forces. However, the president often has the final say on a much wider range of matters. (See pages 20–23 on President Vladimir Putin.)

SECOND IN COMMAND

The prime minister is the head of the government. The various public organisations such as the ministries of education and health are accountable to the prime minister. The prime minister controls policies on issues relating to labour (work) and family, and makes sure that the president's policies are carried out. (See pages 24–25 on Prime Minister Dmitry Medvedev.)

★ The White House is the main government building in Moscow.

HOW WAS RUSSIA GOVERNED IN THE PAST?

Russia has been a democracy for only a very short period in its long history. For most of the twentieth century it was a communist state. Before that, it was a monarchy, ruled by a long line of kings called tsars.

THE LIFE OF THE TSARS

The rule of the tsars began in 1547, when Ivan IV ('the Terrible') established the Tsardom of Russia. It became a huge empire stretching across Europe, Asia and North America. For most of this period of monarchy, control was in the hands of one family – the Romanovs – who ruled as autocrats, allowing no challenge to their power. A massive divide grew up between the wealthy ruling elite and the Russian people, who laboured in poverty on their lords' estates.

THE 1905 REVOLUTION

In 1905, years of bad government drove the Russian people to demand change. Across the country, soviets were established – local councils run along socialist lines. Workers went on strike. People demanded a constitutional monarchy. Tsar Nicholas II agreed to form a law-making body called the Duma. But change was slow, and people grew disillusioned.

On 'Bloody Sunday' in 1905, soldiers opened fire on workers marching in protest. More than 100 were killed.

THE 1917 REVOLUTION

In 1914, the First World War broke out and Russia joined Britain, France and their allies in fighting Germany. The war brought more hardship to the Russian people. They blamed Tsar Nicholas and, when revolution broke out again in February 1917, he was forced to abdicate. The Provisional Government failed to control a poverty-stricken country still fighting a war.

In July 1918, Nicholas II, his wife and their five children were executed by the Bolsheviks. Five hundred years of tsarist rule came to a violent end.

'PEACE, LAND AND BREAD'

A second revolution in October 1917 put the Bolsheviks in power. The Bolsheviks were a faction of the Communist Party who appealed to the people with their campaign slogans of 'peace, land and bread' and 'All power to the soviets'. After their victory, the Bolshevik leader, Vladimir Lenin, withdrew the country from the First World War and began sharing land among the Russian peasants.

Bolshevik leader Lenin had spent years in exile in Siberia before returning to mastermind the October Revolution in 1917.

★ LENIN'S RISE

As a young man, Lenin read about a form of communism called Marxism and started to believe that this was the best type of government. He became a revolutionary, plotting against the tsarist government. After the tsar was overthrown, Lenin demanded that Russia should have a government that would truly work in the interests of the people. With the Bolshevik victory in the October Revolution, Lenin became Russia's leader.

REDS VS. WHITES

Despite their success, disagreements simmered between the Bolsheviks and other political groups, including the Socialist Revolutionaries in the government, and the Mensheviks – less radical communists. From 1918 to 1920, political and ideological unrest also played out as a bitter civil war between the Bolsheviks (the Reds), under the command of Leon Trotsky, and anti-communist soldiers (the Whites). When the Bolsheviks emerged victorious in 1920, their complete control was assured. For the next 70 years, Russia was a communist country.

ONE PARTY FOR THE PEOPLE?

Socialism and communism are both based on the idea of a 'classless' society, in which wealth is shared equally between all people. Although this sounds fair, history has shown that such systems can limit the freedom of ordinary people. The government owns all land and property, which puts it in a position of great power. No other political parties are allowed, so there is no one to challenge the communist leadership.

★ Trotsky had helped win the October Revolution and was a key government minister. Many thought he would take over when Lenin died, but Joseph Stalin manoeuvred his way to the top position instead.

In 1922, Russia became the Union of Soviet Socialist Republics (USSR). It was structured as a group of republics (15 at its height), mostly regions of the former Russian Empire. Russia was the largest republic. Real power – and the central government – was in Moscow. Although the republics got to vote members to the Soviet of Nationalities, in reality the Communist Party of the Soviet Union (CPSU) dictated the candidates. In particular, the Party's policy-making body, the Politburo, had great influence.

LIFE UNDER STALIN

When Lenin died in 1924 his successor, Joseph Stalin, immediately set about establishing total control over every aspect of Russian life and government. He used his secret police and terror tactics to rule the country as a dictator for nearly 30 years. He introduced many economic policies that still have an effect in modern Russia. In particular, his series of Five-Year Plans transformed Russian industry and agriculture. Under Stalin's tight control, the USSR later became a global superpower.

★ To help grow enough food, Stalin introduced 'collectivisation'. Farmers had to join their land into one big farm, which everyone worked on collectively.

WHY DID COMMUNISM END?

After the Second World War (1939–45), Stalin made sure that his country got its share of the spoils. But as the Soviet sphere of influence grew, democracies in the West began to fear the spread of communism and the increasing power of the USSR.

THE COLD WAR

From 1947 to 1991, there was a period of ideological conflict between the USA and the Soviet Union – the world's two great superpowers. This became known as the Cold War (rather than a 'hot' war in which fighting took place). Most notably, both countries began a race to develop and stockpile nuclear weapons.

WARMING UP

Stalin's harsh rule ended with his death in 1953. His successor, Nikita Khrushchev, made many changes within Russia in a process that became known as 'de-Stalinisation'. He allowed groups such as Koreans and Poles, which had been driven out by Stalin, back into the country. And Khrushchev's agricultural policies were successful – for a while at least.

★ After the Second World War, Germany was split into the democratic West Germany and the socialist, Soviet-influenced East Germany. The Berlin Wall was a visible sign of this 'Iron Curtain' between the spheres of influence.

Khrushchev met with US President John F. Kennedy in 1961 in the hope that the two superpowers could co-exist more peacefully.

ECONOMIC PROBLEMS

Khrushchev's opponents forced him to step down in 1964. As Leonid Brezhnev emerged as the USSR's new leader, the government clamped down again. Freedom of speech was limited and the press was censored. Brezhnev spent a great deal of money on building nuclear weapons – and the USSR began to face economic problems.

MODERN COMMUNISM

In 1985, Mikhail Gorbachev became head of the Communist Party. Although he was a fervent believer in communism, Gorbachev also recognised the need for reform. He called for more openness in government ('Glasnost'). His policy of Perestroika ('restructuring') changed the way the economy and industry were organised. Gorbachev allowed ordinary people greater freedoms, but this opened the door to protests for further reform. Some Soviet republics began demanding independence from Russia.

'[Russia] is a riddle, wrapped in mystery inside an enigma.'

Winston Churchill, wondering which side Russia would support in the Second World War

Gorbachev's policies were very popular, marking a change from the long years of fear and repression.

END OF AN ERA

Gorbachev's economic policies undermined some key principles of communism. In 1991, a group tried to restore full communist control, but the tide of change could not be turned back. In July, the first democratic elections since 1917 were held, and Gorbachev lost power to Boris Yeltsin. Yeltsin was sympathetic to the demands of nationalist movements in the republics. As, one by one, they declared independence, the USSR began to disintegrate. It was formally dissolved on 26 December 1991.

★ While working under Gorbachev, Yeltsin had felt that even greater reform was needed.

A NEW RUSSIA

In its place, a new state emerged: the Russian Federation. The fledgling country was going to be built on democratic ideals, but this was no simple task. Although it had lost much of its territory, it was still the largest country in the world – and it was in a state of near-total collapse. How could the government transform the country from its communist-style economy to a full market economy built on private ownership and the free exchange of goods? It took years to implement these changes, and some of them had long-lasting effects.

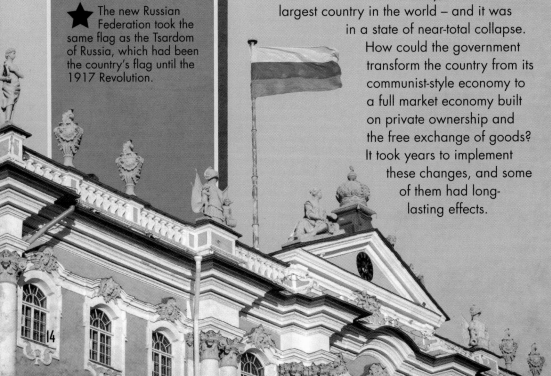

★ The new Russian Federation took the same flag as the Tsardom of Russia, which had been the country's flag until the 1917 Revolution.

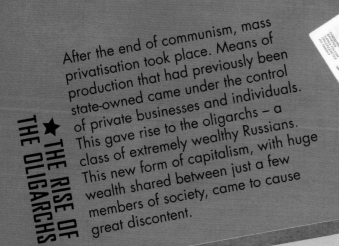

THE RISE OF THE OLIGARCHS ★

After the end of communism, mass privatisation took place. Means of production that had previously been state-owned came under the control of private businesses and individuals. This gave rise to the oligarchs – a class of extremely wealthy Russians. This new form of capitalism, with huge wealth shared between just a few members of society, came to cause great discontent.

THE CONSTITUTION OF 1993

Yeltsin's first years in power were also plagued by questions over exactly what type of democracy Russia should be. Who should have the final say – parliament or the president? Eventually, in 1993, the Constitution of the Russian Federation was agreed and the country became a presidential republic. The constitution outlined the rights of the Russian people, including affordable housing, pensions and free healthcare. But the constitution also gave the president significant powers over policy and political appointments. This has left the system exposed to problems.

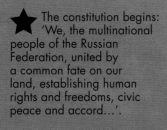

★ The constitution begins: 'We, the multinational people of the Russian Federation, united by a common fate on our land, establishing human rights and freedoms, civic peace and accord…'.

GOVERNMENT STRUCTURED?

The word 'federal' refers to the fact that Russia has a mixed form of government. That is, the country has a central (national or federal) government, plus a series of regional governments. This effectively creates two 'levels' of government that are designed to work together in a single political system.

SUBJECTS OF THE FEDERATION

The Russian Federation is made up of 83 administrative regions, which all have a degree of self-government. There are different names for the types of region – including oblast, republic, kray and okrug – but they are all equal subjects of the Russian Federation. Each of these areas has its own elected legislature.

★ Most people of non-Russian ethnic backgrounds live in the republics. Groups, such as the Yakut (pictured), often have their own culture and traditions.

SOME SELF-GOVERNMENT

For a country the size of Russia, a federal system seems a logical form of government. Large parts of it are populated by different nationalities, often with different languages and cultures. The system means that different areas can manage their own affairs. In the years after the Russian Federation was established, the administrative regions enjoyed the autonomy granted to them by the 1993 constitution.

WHO'S REALLY IN CHARGE?

In 2000, however, the central government established several new districts that were not agreed by the constitution. Each of these 'federal districts' had a special envoy appointed by the new president, Vladimir Putin. The balance of power in Russia began to lean more heavily towards the central government again – and the president in particular.

People demonstrated for and against the Russian annexation of the Crimea. These demonstrators support President Putin's action.

SEIZING NEW LAND

In 2014, Russia seized the Crimea region from Ukraine and made it a new federal district. The majority of people in the Crimea are ethnic Russians, and they voted in a referendum to become part of Russia. The government of Ukraine and most countries in the West regard Russia's action as illegal. They do not recognise the Crimea as part of Russia.

THREE BRANCHES

So, how does the central system in Moscow work? There are three branches to the Russian government. The Executive is the president and the prime minister – the key decision-makers. The Legislature is the Russian parliament, the body that proposes and passes laws. The Judiciary is the branch that ensures those laws are carried out. It comprises the courts and judges.

TWO HOUSES

As in many democracies, the Russian parliament has two separate 'houses'. The upper house is the Federation Council. It has 170 members – representatives chosen by local politicians from each of Russia's administrative divisions. The State Duma is the lower house of parliament. Its 450 members are elected by a national public vote for a five-year term.

The Federation Council represents the rights and needs of all the different administrative regions of Russia.

★ The chairman of the State Duma oversees its day-to-day affairs. Chairman Vyacheslav Volodin (right) is pictured here with Vladimir Putin.

PASSING LAWS

Laws have to be approved by both houses. A bill is first presented to the Duma. If the Duma passes it, the bill moves up to discussion in the Federation Council. Even if a bill is passed by both houses, the president holds the power of veto, which means he can refuse to allow the bill to become law.

MANY PARTIES

In contrast to its one-party communist days, there are now several political parties in Russia. However, the success of a party has often been based on what people think of its leader, rather than on its policies and practices. Holding the most seats in the State Duma, the current ruling party is United Russia – the party that the president and prime minister belong to. Other parties include the Communist Party, the Liberal Democratic Party of Russia and A Just Russia.

'We have gone through major challenging transformations, and were able to overcome new and extremely complex economic and social challenges, preserved the unity of our country, built a democratic society and set it on the path to freedom and independence.'

President Vladimir Putin, 2018

President Vladimir Putin is the most powerful person in the country. He controls the Russian government, dictates policy and chooses Russia's most important officials. In his role as either president or prime minister, Putin has been the key figure in Russian politics since his election in 2000.

LIFE IN THE COLD WAR

Putin was born in Leningrad (now called St Petersburg) in 1952, and later studied law there. In 1985, he joined Russia's secret security and spy agency, the KGB. He worked for this organisation in the German city of Dresden, which was part of Soviet-controlled East Germany at the time (see page 12). In 1990, with the USSR on the verge of collapse, Putin returned to Russia.

★ Putin's wife Lyudmila and daughter went with him to Dresden, and a second daughter was born while they were there. Putin and Lyudmila divorced in 2014.

'I come from an ordinary family, and this is how I lived for a long time, nearly my whole life. I lived as an average, normal person and I have always maintained that connection.'

Vladimir Putin

POLITICS AND POLICING

Putin became advisor to the mayor of St Petersburg in 1990 and later became deputy mayor. In 1996, he joined President Yeltsin's staff and in 1998 Yeltsin made him director of the KGB's successor organisation, the FSB. From there Putin became secretary of the Security Council, an extremely influential organisation overseen directly by the president.

As chairman of St Petersburg's Foreign Relations Committee, Putin (far right) helped to host a visit from Gorbachev in 1994.

PRIME MINISTER, PART I

Although Putin wasn't widely known outside the government at the time, Yeltsin decided that Putin should be his heir as president. In preparation for this, Putin was made prime minister in August 1999. In this role, he earned a reputation for getting things done.

★ Yeltsin (left) recognised Putin's leadership abilities and made him prime minister. Six months later, Putin was president.

★ PARLIAMENTARY APPROVAL

The president chooses the prime minister he wants. The constitution states that the Duma is allowed to veto his decision, so in theory its members get a say in who is the parliamentary leader. But if the Duma rejects the president's choice three times, he can dissolve parliament and call new elections.

A POPULAR PRESIDENT

On 31 December 1999, Yeltsin stepped down as president. Three months later, Putin secured 53 per cent of the vote and stepped into the role. He inherited a weak and divided Russia, and one of his first moves was to establish seven federal districts to assert greater control over the country (see page 17). As the Russian people saw him tackling corruption and trying to reduce the power of the wealthy oligarchs, he became increasingly popular.

PROBLEMS IN CHECHNYA

One of the biggest challenges Putin faced was the battle for independence in the republic of Chechnya. The conflict continued for several years, and after a Russian military campaign to supress the rebels, there were bitter revenge attacks. In one incident, a group of Chechens attacked a theatre in Moscow and 130 people were killed. In 2003, Chechnya agreed to stay as part of Russia on condition that it received greater powers of self-government. Despite this, some Chechens still want independence.

★ Thousands of Russian soldiers were sent to Chechnya to fight the Chechen guerrilla rebels.

SPEAKING OUT ON WORLD AFFAIRS

President Putin condemned the 9/11 terrorist attacks on the USA, but he did not support the British and US invasion of Iraq that followed those attacks. He believed that these actions were 'shaking the foundations of global stability and international law'. Such signs of strength, along with improvements in the Russian economy in his first term as president, ensured that Putin was easily re-elected in 2004.

★ More than 1,000 people were arrested in protests during the election in December 2011.

PRIME MINISTER TO PRESIDENT

After two terms as president, Putin couldn't run again in 2008. His prime minister, Dmitry Medvedev, became president, and immediately chose Putin as his prime minister. The two men swapped jobs again in 2012, but this was not such an easy election. Some groups accused Putin's party, United Russia, of vote-rigging, and there were widespread protests. Many people were arrested, including the leader of the opposition Progress Party, Alexei Navalny. Putin won the election, and six years later he scored a second term with 77.5 per cent of the vote.

Putin was named the most powerful man in the world by *Forbes* magazine four years running from 2013.

★ MANAGED DEMOCRACY

Some commentators have pointed out that Putin has changed the nature of democracy in Russia. They say that in the years since his first election, he has gradually implemented a system of 'managed democracy'. This is where elections seem outwardly democratic, but are in fact largely determined by the ruling party. Some see this as a sign of how powerful Putin has become.

The current prime minister of Russia is Dmitry Medvedev. Over nearly 20 years, Medvedev and Putin have built a strong partnership. With the two men switching roles when necessary, it may seem that they have shared power fairly equally. But some claim that even during Medvedev's time as president, Putin really kept control.

PUTIN'S CHOICE

Like Putin, Medvedev was born in St Petersburg (then Leningrad), in 1965. Putin and Medvedev met while they were both working with Anatoly Sobchak, the mayor of St Petersburg. When Yeltsin tipped Putin for his successor, Medvedev ran Putin's campaign in 2000 to secure the presidency. Putin made Medvedev his chief of staff, then appointed him as first deputy prime minister.

MEDVEDEV FOR PRESIDENT

As prime minister, Medvedev earned a reputation as a reformer. His enjoyment of Western culture led him to encourage Western-style changes within Russia. When Putin named Medvedev his successor as president, he won the 2008 election easily. Despite their close working relationship, Medvedev was less conservative than Putin. As president, he talked about the need for Russia to modernise. He never got the chance to implement these ideas, though – in 2012 he stepped down to allow Putin back into the driving seat.

The role-sharing between Putin and Medvedev has been described as a 'tandemocracy'.

A CONTROVERSIAL FIGURE

Medvedev has been prime minister again since 2012. But in recent years he has come under fire from critics. In 2017, Alexei Navalny (see page 23) accused the prime minister of corruption, including taking bribes from the oligarchs. Some people began to fear that Medvedev's unpopularity was negatively affecting the president. A poll in January 2019 revealed that Putin's approval ratings had dropped and that the Russian people were unhappy with Medvedev's government. Commentators speculated whether it was time Putin ended this close relationship.

As president, Medvedev allowed more liberal ideas to come under discussion. Putin changed direction on this when he was re-elected in 2012.

★ In early 2019, the president's 'trust' rating was only 33 per cent. Experts think that the accusations of misconduct against Medvedev are to blame for this.

'Freedom is a unique concept that everyone interprets differently.'

Dmitry Medvedev in his final interview as president, 2012

WHAT ARE TODAY'S KEY CHALLENGES?

President Putin campaigned and won on principles of stability and tradition. After years of difficulties under the communist regime, it is not hard to see why this appealed to the Russian people in 2000 – or why it still does today. But the president has his work cut out in dealing with the challenges Russia still faces.

A BETTER LIFE

One effect of an unstable economy is that people may leave the country, and this is a particular problem in Russia. Every year, thousands of young people are moving from Russia to other countries in search of better jobs and greater economic stability. In the decade from 2000 to 2010, more than 1.25 million Russians emigrated. The consequence of this is an ageing population and declining birth rate. The government needs to find ways of dealing with depopulation, as well as social issues such as poverty.

★ Even with a university degree, young people in Russia can find it hard to get a job that pays enough to make ends meet.

THE EFFECTS OF CORRUPTION

Experts believe that corruption has
infiltrated many areas of Russian life.
This may range from government officials
taking money from big businesses, to
police officers accepting bribes to walk
away from traffic violations. Reports
suggest that corruption may be affecting
sectors such as healthcare, education and
housing. In countries where corruption is
found in these areas, it stops the economy
functioning the way it should.

★ Corruption puts
a strain on the
economy and society.

FOREIGN RELATIONS

Some countries have criticised what
they see as President Putin's increasingly
conservative policies. Putin does not
always believe that foreign values and
interests are aligned with Russia's own.
Sometimes, when foreign countries
disapprove of international actions
Russia takes, they impose trade
sanctions. These can have a
devastating effect on the Russian
economy. Finding ways to get
along in the international
community is vital for
resolving both international
and domestic issues.

★ Since President Putin ordered
the annexation of the Crimea
in 2014, the USA and the EU have
operated sanctions against Russia.

★ RANKING CORRUPTION

Each year, an organisation called Transparency International
publishes the 'Corruption Perceptions Index'. This scores
countries by how corrupt they are perceived to be, from
0 (highly corrupt) to 100 (very clean). In the 2018 index,
Russia scored 28. That gave it a ranking of 138th out of 180
countries on the index. Transparency International rates any
country with a score lower than 30 as an 'autocratic regime'.

WHY ARE ENVIRONMENTAL ISSUES IMPORTANT?

During the Soviet era, Russia experienced widespread and rapid industrialisation. At the time, people were only concerned with stabilising the economy – no one appeared to be worried about the environmental impact of all that industry. It's now clear that pollution and nuclear waste created years ago have had long-term effects.

THE SILVER LINING TO GLOBAL WARMING?

The situation is worsening as air and water pollution contribute to global warming. In fact, Russia is warming two and a half times faster than anywhere else in the world. Campaigners say this is why the government needs to make environmental issues a high priority. But there are economic advantages to global warming for Russia. Melting ice caps may eventually open up shipping routes in the north that would allow Russia to trade more easily with countries such as China. And if the Arctic permafrost is reduced, Russia may be able to extract oil and gas from currently inaccessible parts of Siberia.

★ Despite being the world's fourth-largest emitter of greenhouse gases, Russia has only committed to limiting a *rise* in its emissions.

DEFORESTATION

Russia is home to 19 per cent of the world's remaining forest reserves. This places a huge responsibility on the country to protect and maintain its forest areas. But illegal logging is a particular problem. Deforestation in Russia accounts for 20–40 per cent of the 1.5 billion tonnes of carbon dioxide that are lost globally to deforestation every year.

★ Russia's deforestation rates are alarmingly high considering how much of the global total it is responsible for.

ENERGY ISSUES

Only 3.6 per cent of Russia's energy comes from renewable resources. This is low compared to other industrialised nations. However, the government's Decree 449 (2013) created a structure for developing more renewable power projects. The International Renewable Energy Agency believes that this will bring Russia's renewable energy consumption up to 11.3 per cent by 2030.

'An increase of two or three degrees wouldn't be so bad for a northern country like Russia. We could spend less on fur coats, and the grain harvest would go up.'

Vladimir Putin, 2003

Although Russia makes use of its plentiful water to create hydropower, there is still a lot more potential for harnessing this resource.

★ HYDROPOWER

There is one area of renewable energy that Russia has proved open to – and very successful in. This is hydropower. The country now has 102 hydropower plants, generating energy from water. It ranks fifth in the world for hydropower production, and there are plans for expansion of this renewable industry.

WHAT RESOURCES DOES RUSSIA HAVE?

Russia's vast reserves of oil, natural gas and minerals have the potential to bring the country huge wealth. But taking full advantage of these resources requires a lot of experts and infrastructure.

THE IMPORTANCE OF OIL

Russia has been slow to get on board with renewables because it is so rich in fossil fuels. With oil and natural gas beneath its feet, there's little incentive to look elsewhere for resources. Russia produces more oil than any other country in the world. It is also second only to Saudi Arabia in exporting its oil to other countries.

★ Many of Russia's oil fields are in the freezing landscapes of Siberia.

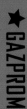 ★ **GAZPROM** Natural gas company Gazprom is mostly owned by the Russian government. It is the business world's biggest oil producer thanks to the largest natural gas field in the world, the Shtokman field. Gazprom employs nearly 470,000 people and brings in revenue of US$112 billion a year. It provides more than 5 per cent of Russia's gross domestic product (GDP), which gives the government huge power.

NATURAL GAS

Russia also has the largest reserves of natural gas and is the world's leading gas exporter. Currently, 76 per cent of Russia's gas is sold to the European Union. To diversify the industry, in 2014 Russia agreed a 30-year energy deal with China. This will be a boost to the Russian economy – but there are drawbacks. To fulfil China's needs, Russia has had to establish new gas fields, not to mention building a 3,000-km long pipeline to carry the gas to China!

★ Work began on the Chinese section of the gas pipeline in 2015.

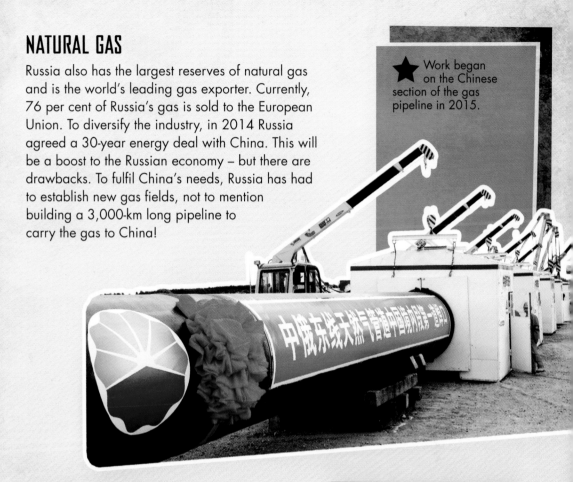

PRECIOUS METALS

The wealth in Russia's rocks is not confined to oil and gas. Metals such as gold, copper, aluminium and iron ore, and minerals including diamonds and phosphate are all abundant. The mining industry is the second largest in the country, after oil and gas. While the government has a vested interest in oil and gas, most mining companies are privately owned. Only the diamond-mining giant Alrosa is partly state-owned.

★ In January 2019, Russia's gold reserves were reported to have reached an all-time high of 2,119 tonnes.

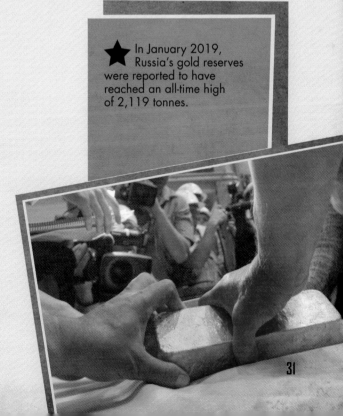

WHAT ABOUT THE ECONOMY?

According to the World Bank, in 2018 Russia ranked 57th in the world in terms of GDP per head. The Russian government must constantly find ways to keep the economy growing and stave off economic threats.

RELIANCE ON RESOURCES

Owning resources that the rest of the world needs is good for the economy. However, it also makes Russia vulnerable to global economic changes. Saudi Arabia and the USA have jostled with Russia for first place as oil producer for years. If other countries also become global oil suppliers, Russia's economy may suffer. Even now, global variations in the price of oil can have a huge effect on the Russian government's income.

★ This is a huge oil refinery in Tyumen. In total, Russia's natural resources contribute 60 per cent of its GDP.

TOUGH CHOICES

With so many provinces across such a huge territory, the Russian economy is extremely regionalised. But the majority of wealth is generated in just a handful of areas (one-fifth in Moscow). It is not always easy to make sure that money gets to the right places. In times of economic difficulty, the central government has tough choices to make about where to focus its spending – on national or regional needs.

TRADING WITH THE WORLD

During Putin's first two terms as president he resisted joining the World Trade Organization (WTO), which oversees international trading rules and agreements. The president did not want to encourage Western influence in Russia. However, Medvedev thought differently and brought Russia into the WTO in 2012. Russia now has greater access to goods from other countries, and pays less to import them. Membership of the WTO has also opened up new markets for Russian goods.

★ Russia relies on its trucking industry to carry goods to its far-flung regions. A 2015 truckers' strike against a new road tax caused economic problems for the country.

During the 2014 oil price drop, the cost of goods being imported by Russia also rose. This caused severe inflation.

THE PRICE OF OIL

★ In 2014, oil prices around the world fell dramatically. Russia had to drop its own prices to compete in the global market, but this had a serious effect on the economy. The value of the Russian currency, the ruble, dropped 59 per cent against the US dollar in just six months.

WHAT IS RUSSIA'S NUCLEAR STATUS?

In 1949, Russia became the second country in the world (after the USA) to develop nuclear weapons. Throughout the Cold War years, the threat of nuclear war between the superpowers kept the world on tenterhooks. Since the 1990s, many countries have reduced their nuclear weapons, including Russia. However, it remains a serious nuclear presence.

A NUCLEAR STATE

The Treaty on the Non-Proliferation of Nuclear Weapons is an international agreement set up in 1968. It was designed to stop the spread of nuclear weapons and encourage disarmament. The treaty recognises five 'nuclear states' – signatories to the agreement that have developed nuclear weapons – the USA, the UK, France, China and Russia. Four other countries also have nuclear weapons (India, Pakistan, North Korea and Israel), but they have not signed the agreement.

★ At its Cold War peak, Russia had an estimated 40,000 nuclear warheads.

ARMS CONTROL

For years, Russia willingly participated in discussions about nuclear weapons control. It made several agreements with the USA. These resulted in a big reduction in its nuclear arsenal to an estimated 4,350 warheads. But the relationship between Russia and the USA has worsened in recent years, and one of the casualties has been nuclear co-operation.

'We are not aiming for an advantage, we are aiming to retain balance and to provide for our own safety.'

Vladimir Putin, on nuclear weapons, 2018

In 2019, the USA and Russia both withdrew from a 1987 nuclear treaty, accusing each other of violating the agreement. There were protests like the one pictured in many countries. This one was in Germany.

A NEW START

In April 2010, Russia and the USA signed New START (Strategic Arms Reduction Treaty). Both nations agreed to reduce their operational warheads and launchers. In 2019 however, the USA claimed that at the time, Russia had insisted that the treaty only cover a small group of weapons. The USA has said it will begin discussions with China over a new nuclear reduction deal.

★ This Russian supersonic 'interceptor' jet carries an air-launched hypersonic missile. Such missiles could be armed with nuclear warheads.

★ HYPERSONIC MISSILES In 2019, the Russian defence minister Sergei Shoigu announced that the country was planning to develop a new type of hypersonic missile. These are missiles that travel so fast they cannot be stopped by any known missile defence system. This could trigger an arms race between Russia, the USA and China, and with countries in Europe within range of the missiles.

WHAT ABOUT HUMAN RIGHTS?

The Russian constitution outlines the basic rights and freedoms that all its citizens should enjoy. It is the president's job as 'guarantor' of the constitution to ensure that these rights are upheld. But there is evidence that over the years of Putin's presidency, some rights and freedoms have been curtailed.

POLITICAL PERSECUTION

Democracy seemed to offer a chance for open political dialogue as opposed to the persecution of the communist era. But since Putin took office there have been increasing signs of a clampdown on political opposition. Most notably, in December 2017 the Russian Supreme Court upheld a ban on Alexei Navalny standing in elections. The European Court of Human Rights has called the Russian government's treatment of Navalny 'unlawful' and 'politically motivated'.

'All forms of limitations of human rights on social, racial, national, linguistic or religious grounds shall be banned.'

Article 19 of the Russian Constitution

Despite being arrested and imprisoned numerous times, Navalny continues to encourage opposition to President Putin's government.

WOMEN'S RIGHTS

Women do not always enjoy equal status to men. Only 13 out of 170 members of the Federation Council are women, and 61 out of 450 in the Duma. This means that women don't have an equal voice in policy-making. In 2017 domestic violence in Russia was decriminalised, which has been seen as a move against women, who are the majority of victims.

Бьет – значит любит

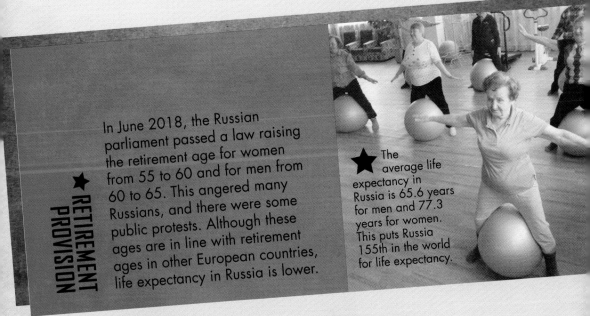

RETIREMENT PROVISION

In June 2018, the Russian parliament passed a law raising the retirement age for women from 55 to 60 and for men from 60 to 65. This angered many Russians, and there were some public protests. Although these ages are in line with retirement ages in other European countries, life expectancy in Russia is lower.

★ The average life expectancy in Russia is 65.6 years for men and 77.3 years for women. This puts Russia 155th in the world for life expectancy.

MEDIA CONTROL

The state runs most Russian TV channels, and the news usually shows the government in a positive light. Newspapers mostly support government policies. Journalists may risk attack if they report corruption or human rights abuses. In one infamous case in 2006, the journalist Anna Politkovskaya was shot dead. People had called her 'unpatriotic' because she had criticised President Putin's campaign in Chechnya.

DIGITAL FREEDOMS

President Putin has initiated a series of restrictions on digital media, and a 2018 report suggested that internet freedom in Russia had declined for six years running. Websites are censored and the use of virtual private networks (VPNs) has been limited. Bloggers with more than 3,000 daily readers have to register with a regulator, who monitors their content.

HOW DOES RUSSIA EXERT A GLOBAL INFLUENCE?

It is no surprise that the largest country in the world should have a big influence on global affairs. President Putin has made every effort to consolidate and extend Russia's status on the world stage.

PUBLIC OPINION

A 2018 survey of 25 countries showed that international opinion of Russia was low. Sixty-three per cent of people said they had no confidence that President Putin would do the right thing in international affairs. However, the same survey suggested that Russia's global influence is increasing. Forty-two per cent said Russia's role on the world stage is more important now than it was ten years ago.

THE SYRIAN CRISIS

In 2011, civil war broke out in Syria after anti-government protests were put down with force. In 2015, Russia stepped in to help the Syrian government. Sending forces to Syria sent a message to the world that Russia was a key player in the Middle East, and increased its global status. But the USA claims that Russian airstrikes have killed thousands of Syrian civilians. Russia's intervention there has divided international opinion.

★ In the 2018 survey, 81 per cent of Russians expressed confidence in President Putin.

★ Russia said the airstrikes in Syria were against the militant group Islamic State. But the USA claimed they were aimed at Syrian anti-government groups

VETOES IN THE UN

The situation in Syria is one of the issues over which Russia has flexed its muscles in the United Nations Security Council. Between 2011 and 2018, it vetoed 12 resolutions put forward by the council to deal with the problems in Syria. Some experts argue that Russia's decisions further its own interests. However, others argue that this is just the way that international politics plays out. For example, the USA has a worse record than Russia for blocking UN resolutions.

'Our soldiers are there in order to secure Russia's interests in this critically important part of the world, which is so near to us. And they will stay there, for as long as it is in Russia's interest for them to do so.'

Vladimir Putin, June 2018

Russia's status as a permanent member of the UN gives it great control over international affairs.

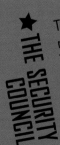

THE SECURITY COUNCIL

★ The Security Council is the part of the United Nations responsible for ensuring international peace and security. There are 15 members of the UNSC. Ten of these change every two years, but five countries have a permanent seat – China, France, the UK, the USA and Russia. As a permanent member, Russia can block any actions put forward by the international community that it disagrees with.

WHAT ARE RUSSIA'S INTERNATIONAL RELATIONS LIKE?

The signing of the gas deal with China in 2014 (see page 31) is an indication of the shifting geopolitical landscape. As Russia's relationship with the West grows more strained, the government is trying to make new friends in other parts of the world. Asia, on Russia's doorstep, is the obvious place to look.

CHINA

Despite being the two major communist powers for most of the twentieth century, a mutual distrust existed between Russia and China for many years. Since the fall of the USSR, though, the two countries have co-operated in several ways. As well as the gas deal, the state-owned Russian nuclear power company Rosatom has agreed to build four nuclear power plants in China. In June 2019, President Putin and President Xi Jinping made more than US$20 billion worth of deals to improve economic ties between their countries.

★ President Putin with Chinese president Xi Jinping. Together these Eastern powers present a formidable opposition to what they see as Western dominance in global affairs.

NORTH KOREA

In the Soviet era, the USSR was an ally of communist North Korea. The relationship worsened after the fall of the USSR, but now President Putin is trying to strengthen ties as another bolster against declining relations with the West. In April 2019, he met with North Korean leader Kim Jong-un to discuss North Korea's nuclear programme and other issues.

'They [the North Koreans] only need guarantees about their security. That's it. All of us together need to think about this.'

Vladimir Putin, after talks with North Korean leader Kim Jong-un

★ Unlike the USA, President Putin was not seeking disarmament during the 2019 talks with Kim Jong-un, but the 'stabilisation' of nuclear development.

FORMER SOVIET STATES

For some years after the end of the USSR, Russia retained an influence over former communist states in eastern Europe. As these new countries found their own way in the world, that influence declined. Russia's annexation of the Crimea (see page 17) is an example of 'hard power', but Russia also wants to regain some of that traditional influence with 'soft power' – using persuasion and nostalgia to encourage economic, political and social alliances.

Energy agreements are one way that Russia exerts control over former Soviet states. Subsidising fuels and building infrastructure, such as pipelines, in these countries keeps them on side.

RUSSIA AND THE USA AT ODDS

Since the end of the Cold War, the relationship between Russia and the USA has swung back and forth between conflict and co-operation. During Barack Obama's time as president of the USA, he and President Putin worked together to address issues such as the situation in Syria, but commentators noted that the two men seemed to have little respect for each other.

During the 2016 Summer Olympics, it was discovered that the Russian state had sanctioned doping among Russian athletes to improve their performance. The event saw international opinion of Russia drop to an all-time low.

INTERFERING INTERNATIONALLY

Russia was accused of interfering in the 2016 US elections to help Donald Trump to the presidency. The Russian government has been dismissive of the claims, but there is a pattern of alleged Russian interference in foreign politics. For example, the Italian deputy prime minister, Matteo Salvini, was accused of receiving funding from Russian businesses to help his party's campaign for the European Parliament.

HELSINKI 2018 · HELSINKI 2018

★ Putin has described the relationship between Russia and the USA as getting 'worse and worse'. The USA now regards Russia as a 'strategic competitor'.

'The USA is a great power. Probably the only superpower in existence today. We accept that and we are ready to work together with them. What we don't need is for them to get involved in our affairs, tell us how to live our lives, and prevent Europe from building a relationship with us.'

Vladimir Putin, at the St Petersburg Economic Forum, June 2016

RELATIONSHIP WITH THE UK

In 2018, President Putin said 'In my mind, UK-Russian relations are at a dead end'. One reason for this was the poisoning of former Soviet double agent Sergei Skripal and his daughter Yulia in the UK in 2018. British police believe that the attack may have been committed by Russian military intelligence. The government initially denied any involvement, and President Putin later said 'We need to forget about all this'. The UK is Russia's biggest business investor, so it is important to find a way out of this 'dead end'.

Police had to decontaminate the area where former spy Sergei Skripal and his daughter Yulia were found after the attack, which used a chemical that affects the human nervous system.

WHAT LIES AHEAD?

Less than 30 years have passed since Russia started on the road to democracy. It is not easy to implement a whole new system of government, especially in a country as large as Russia. There have been many positive changes since 1991, but Russia still experiences difficulties, both foreign and domestic. Dealing with these is key to a successful future.

ELECTION PROMISES

Vladimir Putin has effectively controlled Russian politics for 20 years, and his re-election in 2018 secured him another six. A poll in 2019 showed his approval rating at 66 per cent, but he will have to work hard to maintain his popularity. There remains a wide divide between rich and poor in Russia, and people expect the president to deliver on his election promises to deal with issues such as poverty.

★ As Putin progresses through what should be his final term, people are starting to ask who will replace him. Or will he find a way of standing again?

Dealing with social issues such as homelessness and poverty will be key to keeping the support of the Russian people.

The 12 National Projects are President Putin's plan to modernise Russian society and revitalise the economy. They outline key sectors for government investment, which range from healthcare and education to ecology and culture. They include 150 'development goals', and show a shift in priorities from military and defence projects to infrastructure and social concerns such as living conditions.

LETTING OUTSIDERS IN

Membership of the WTO (see page 33) has encouraged foreign companies to invest in Russia, but economic commentators claim that the accusations of corruption are likely to put off many investors. Cleaning up the country's image is an important first step towards economic improvement. Foreign firms seeking to set up in Russia may also have difficulty because of the lack of infrastructure and legal challenges. Addressing these areas will allow Russia to truly open up to outsiders and become a global economy.

LOOKING OUTWARDS

As relations with the West deteriorate, President Putin plans to increase Russia's defences against Western interference. He is also continuing on an increasingly conservative path and isolating Russians from Western influences. This is likely to result in closer relationships with countries in Asia and the Middle East, which will open up Russia to new opportunities and ideas.

'I think that we should raise a new, young generation of leaders, responsible people who will be able to take on the responsibility of Russia.'

Vladimir Putin, on who his successor should be, June 2018

45

GLOSSARY

abdicate
When a monarch gives up the throne.

autocratic
Describing a system of government when one person has complete power and control.

autonomy
The right to self-government.

capitalism
A system of government in which property, business and industry are privately owned, and citizens can work towards making a profit for themselves.

communism
A system of government in which the state owns and controls all property and means of production. Citizens contribute and receive according to their needs.

conservative
Having traditional values and ideas, often to the point of resisting change.

constitutional monarchy
A system of government in which power is shared between a monarch and a government.

decriminalise
To make something that has been banned legal again.

dictator
Someone who rules with complete control, often having taken power by force.

federal
Describing the central government in a system where several states that also maintain some powers of internal government form a union.

FSB
A Russian government organisation responsible for security within the country.

gross domestic product (GDP)
The monetary value of all of a country's goods and services; it is used as a general measure of the state of the economy.

hydropower
Energy generated by harnessing the power of moving water.

ideological
Describing things related to people's political beliefs and ideals.

inflation
A rise in the general cost of goods, so money is worth less.

infrastructure
The systems and services (such as transport and power supplies) that help a country to work effectively.

Marxism
The social system on which communism is based, theorised by Karl Marx, in which people contribute their skills for the good of all, and everyone's welfare is taken care of.

privatisation
When public businesses and industries are sold off to private companies or individuals.

referendum
A vote in which the people of a country or region are invited to make a decision directly about a particular issue.

sanctions
Penalties for disobeying an international law or agreement, when other countries put limits on trade with a particular nation.

socialism
A system of government in which the community owns and controls the means of production. Citizens give and receive according to their ability and needs. Often regarded as a stage between communism and capitalism.

sovereignty
The right of a state or country to govern itself.

sphere of influence
The geographical regions over which a country has political control or influence.

stockpile
Store up a huge collection of something, often weapons.

FURTHER INFORMATION

BOOKS

Russia (The Land and the People), Cath Senker, Wayland, 2018

Russia (Journey Through), Anita Ganeri, Franklin Watts, 2018

Vladimir Putin: President of Russia (World Leaders), Michael Regan, North Star Editions, 2018

Russia and Moscow (Developing World), Philip Steele, Franklin Watts, 2016

20th Century Russia: A Century of Upheaval, Heather Maisner, Franklin Watts, 2016

WEBSITES

www.bbc.co.uk/news/world-europe-17839672
Russia country profile

www.bbc.co.uk/news/world-europe-15047823
A profile of Russia's current president, Vladimir Putin

www.bbc.co.uk/news/world-europe-17840446
A timeline of key events in Russian history

http://government.ru/en/
The official website of the Russian government

www.natgeokids.com/uk/discover/geography/countries/russia-facts/
National Geographic Kids page all about Russia

administrative regions 16, 17, 18
agriculture 11, 12
Alrosa 31
Asia 4, 8, 40, 45

Berlin Wall 12
Bolsheviks 9, 10
borders 4
Brezhnev, Leonid 13

censorship 13, 37
Chechnya 22, 37
China 4, 28, 31, 34, 35, 39, 40
Cold War 12, 20, 34, 42
communism 5, 7, 8, 9, 10, 11,
 12, 13, 14, 15, 19, 26, 36,
 40, 41
Communist Party 7, 9, 11, 13, 19
constitution 6, 7, 15, 17, 21, 36
corruption 22, 25, 27, 37, 45
Crimea 17, 27, 41

deforestation 29
democracy 5, 8, 12, 15, 18, 19,
 23, 36, 44
Duma 8, 18, 19, 21, 37

economy 5, 11, 13, 14, 15, 22,
 26, 27, 28, 31, 32–33, 40, 45
education 7, 27, 45
elections 7, 14, 18, 16, 19, 20,
 21, 22, 23, 24, 25, 36, 44
energy 28, 29, 30, 31, 41
environmental issues 28–29
ethnic groups 5, 16, 17
Europe 4, 8, 35, 37, 41, 43
European Union (EU) 27, 31, 42
exports 30, 31

federal districts 17, 22
Federation Council 18, 19, 37
First World War 9
France 6, 9, 34, 39
freedom of speech 13
FSB 21

Gazprom 30
GDP 30, 32
Germany 9, 12, 20, 35
global warming 28, 29
Gorbachev, Mikhail 13, 14, 21
government structure 16–19

healthcare 7, 15, 27, 45
housing 15, 27
human rights 15, 36–37

industry 5, 11, 13, 28, 31

KGB 20, 21
Khrushchev, Nikita 12, 13
Kim Jong-un 41

Lenin, Vladimir 9, 10, 11
life expectancy 37

Medvedev, Dmitry 7, 23, 24–25,
 33
Mensheviks 10
Middle East 38, 45
minerals 30, 31
monarchy 5, 8
Moscow 4, 5, 7, 11, 18, 22, 32

National Projects 45
natural gas 28, 30, 31, 40
Navalny, Alexei 23, 25, 36
New START 35
Nicholas II, 8, 9
North Korea 4, 34, 41
nuclear weapons 12, 13, 34–35,
 41

Obama, Barack 42
oil 28, 30, 31, 32, 33
oligarchs 15, 22, 25
Olympic Games 42

pipelines 31, 41
Poland 4, 6
political parties 10, 19, 23
Politkovskaya, Anna 37
population 4, 5, 17, 26
poverty 8, 9, 26, 44, 45
president 6, 7, 15, 17, 18, 19,
 20, 21, 22, 23, 24, 25, 26,
 33, 36, 44
prime minister 6, 7, 18, 19, 20,
 21, 23, 24, 25
privatisation 15
Progress Party 23
Putin, Vladimir 7, 17, 19, 20–23,
 24, 25, 26, 27, 29, 33, 35,
 36, 37, 38, 39, 40, 41, 42,
 43, 44, 45

resources 5, 28, 29, 30–31, 32
Revolution of 1905 8
Revolutions of 1917 9, 10, 14
Rosatom 40

Salvini, Matteo 42
sanctions 27
Saudi Arabia 30, 32
Second World War 12, 13
Shoigu, Sergei 35
Siberia 4, 5, 9, 28, 30
size of Russia 4, 5, 14, 17, 32,
 38, 44
Skripal, Sergei and Yulia 43
Sobchak, Anatoly 24
Socialist Revolutionaries 10
soviets 8, 9
St Petersburg 4, 20, 21, 24, 43
Stalin, Joseph 10, 11, 12
Syria 38, 39, 42

trade 27, 28, 33
Transparency International 27
Trotsky, Leon 10
Trump, Donald 42
tsars 8, 9, 14

UK 9, 34, 39, 43
Ukraine 4, 17
United Nations Security Council 39
United Russia 19, 23
USA 12, 22, 27, 32, 34, 35, 38,
 39, 41, 42, 43
USSR 11, 12, 13, 14, 20, 28,
 40, 41

Volodin, Vyacheslav 18
voting 6, 7, 11, 17, 18, 22,
 23, 37

West, the 12, 17, 24, 33, 40,
 41, 45
women's rights 37
World Trade Organization (WTO)
 33, 45

Xi Jinping 40

Yeltsin, Boris 7, 14, 15, 21,
 22, 24

Zyuganov, Grennady 7

CHINA

WHAT makes China unique?
WHAT is communism?
HOW did China's communism change?
WHAT are today's key challenges?
WHO is Xi Jinping?
WHO is Li Keqiang?
WHAT is a one-party state?
WHAT about human rights?

HOW does the government work?
WHY is the army important?
WHAT about the economy?
WHAT influence does China have?
WHAT about global influences?
HOW does Xi Jinping want to govern?
WHAT lies ahead?

NORTH KOREA

WHAT makes North Korea unique?
WHEN was North Korea founded?
WHAT is communism?
WHO are the Kim family?
WHAT is a one-party state?
HOW does the government work?
WHAT is daily life like?

WHAT about human rights?
WHAT about nuclear weapons?
HOW are neighbouring relations?
WHAT about the rest of the world?
WHY is the army important?
WHAT about the economy?
WHAT lies ahead?

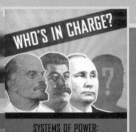

RUSSIA

WHAT makes Russia unique?
WHAT political system does Russia have?
HOW was Russia governed in the past?
WHY did communism end?
HOW is the government structured?
WHO is Vladimir Putin?
WHO is Dmitry Medvedev?
WHAT are today's key challenges?

WHY are environmental issues important?
WHAT resources does Russia have?
WHAT about the economy?
WHAT is Russia's nuclear status?
WHAT about human rights?
HOW does Russia exert a global influence?
WHAT are Russia's international relations like?
WHAT lies ahead?

SAUDI ARABIA

WHAT makes Saudi Arabia unique?
WHO are the Sa'ud family?
WHO is King Salman?
WHO is Mohammed bin Salman?
WHAT is an absolute monarchy?
HOW is the government structured?
WHAT is Sharia law?

WHAT are today's key challenges?
WHAT about human rights?
WHAT about the economy?
WHY is the military important?
WHAT influence does Saudi Arabia have?
WHAT are its global relations like?
WHAT lies ahead?